Systems architecture

Purpose and components of the CPU

- The Central Processing Unit (CPU) works like the brain of the computer and is responsible for carrying out instructions that make software and hardware work.
- The CPU's main responsibilities are to:
  - Carry out instructions from programs
  - Process data inputs from programs and storage
  - Control the rest of the computer system using control signals

Component	Function
Arithmetic Logic Unit (ALU)	• The ALU is responsible for calculations and logic. It performs calculation operations like addition, subtraction, multiplication, and division. • It also makes logical comparisons, like checking if one number is greater than the other or if the two values are equal. • When the CPU needs to decide between things or carry out a calculation, it uses the ALU.
Control Unit (CU)	• The CU tells the rest of the computer how to respond to the instructions it receives. • It manages the flow of data around the CPU and between the CPU and other components like memory or input/output devices. • It sends control signals to other components to coordinate what happens and when, and helps to decode instructions so the CPU knows what action to take.
Cache	• The cache is a small amount of very fast memory located close to or inside the CPU. • It stores frequently used data and instructions, so the CPU doesn't have to keep going back to RAM, which is much slower. This helps the CPU work faster and more efficiently. • There are usually different levels of cache (L1, L2, L3) – the lower the number, the faster and smaller it is.
Registers	• Registers are tiny memory locations within the CPU itself that store small amounts of data temporarily while instructions are being executed. • Registers are the fastest type of memory. • Different registers have different roles – for example, some store memory addresses, others store data being worked on.

Factors affecting CPU performance

Factor	Description	
Clock speed	• The CPU's clock (part of the CU) pulses at fixed intervals to trigger the next action in the CPU. • Clock speed is typically measured in GHz (gigahertz) where 1 GHz = 1 billion cycles per second.	• The faster the clock, the higher the speed at which fetch-execute cycles can take place, therefore more instructions are processed per second.
Cache size	• Cache memory is a small, very fast memory in the CPU that holds frequently used data/instructions as it is quicker to access than data/instructions in RAM. • Cache memory is very expensive, so the average CPU may only have 4MB or 8MB of cache, which is 1000× smaller than 4GB or 8GB of RAM.	• Having a larger cache allows CPUs to hold a larger number of frequently used instructions. This reduces the time it takes to fetch by reducing the time lost whilst waiting to retrieve from RAM.
Number of cores	• Modern CPUs typically have multiple processing cores, each with their own control unit and ALU. They share cache memory and access to other memory. • Common types include dual-core (2 cores) and quad-core (4 cores). • Multi-core CPUs process multiple instructions simultaneously so can increase CPU performance in compatible programs.	• A multi-core CPU with lower clock speed may complete tasks faster (e.g. analysing big data sets like weather patterns, or mining cryptocurrency) than a single-core CPU with a higher clock speed. • However, an increased number of cores can only benefit programs written to utilise multiple cores simultaneously.

Systems architecture

The fetch-execute cycle

- The CPU accomplishes its tasks by running something called the **fetch-execute cycle**, sometimes also called the fetch-decode-execute cycle.
- The faster the CPU can run this cycle, the faster the computer can run tasks. The average computer can run this cycle billions of times a second!

Fetch:
- CPU copies the address of the next instruction from the PC to the MAR.
- Adds to the program counter to point to the next instruction. The instruction at the address is copied from MAR to MDR.

Decode:
- The CU decodes the instruction and signals the appropriate component to 'execute' it.

Execute:
- The instruction is executed by the appropriate component/operation (e.g. ALU may perform a calculation, daqta might be loaded in from RAM).

- **Fetch:**
  - The program counter (PC) holds the address of the next instruction and sends this to memory access register (MAR).
  - The instruction is retrieved from main memory and placed into the memory data register (MDR), and copied to the current instruction register (CIR).
- **Decode:**
  - The control unit (CU) interprets the instruction stored in the CIR.
  - The CU identifies the required operation and the necessary data, registers, or addressing mode.
- **Execute:**
  - The indicated operation is carried out: arithmetic/logic operations (via the ALU), data transfer, or control flow.
  - Results are written back to registers or memory as required.
  - The cycle then repeats for the next instruction.

Von Neumann architecture

- Von Neumann architecture is the name given to a design model for how a computer works. Most modern computers use this. It was created by mathematician John von Neumann in the 1940s.
- Key ideas in Von Neumann architecture:
  - Instructions and data are both stored in the same main memory (RAM).
  - The CPU uses a single bus system to read or write either instructions or data.
  - The computer processes instructions one at a time in the fetch-execute cycle.
- There are 4 key registers that are used in Von Neumann architecture:

Register	Function
Memory Address Register (MAR)	The MAR holds the memory address of the data or instruction that is to be fetched or stored. For example, if the CPU needs to fetch an instruction from address 104, it will place 104 in the MAR.
Memory Data Register (MDR)	The MDR temporarily holds the data that is being fetched or stored in memory. For example, If the CPU is reading from address 104, the data from that address goes into the MDR before it's used.
Program Counter (PC)	The PC stores the address of the next instruction to be fetched. After the instruction is fetched, the PC is usually increased by 1 (so it points to the next instruction in memory). If a jump instruction is used (e.g. in loops), the PC might change to a completely different address.
Accumulator	The accumulator stores intermediate results of calculations carried out by the ALU. For example, if you're adding several numbers together, the result of each calculation is stored here before moving on to the next. Without it, the CPU would have to keep writing results to main memory, which would be much slower.

Computer systems

Types of computer system
- **General purpose systems:** computer systems that can perform a wide range of tasks (e.g. PCs, Macs, tablets, smartphones).
- **Dedicated systems:** computer systems that are designed to perform a specific function (e.g. printers, WiFi routers).
- **Embedded systems:** computer systems built into another device to support its function (e.g. computer systems in washing machines and dishwashers).
  - Embedded systems are primarily intended to monitor and control the various components in the host device (e.g. a dishwasher requires this computer to keep track of water temperature and pressure, washing programs, and timings).
  - These systems are beneficial because their limited range of tasks make them cheap to produce, energy efficient, and very reliable. However, they are only designed to perform specific tasks and are hard to update once manufactured.

Automated systems
- An automated system is a computer-controlled setup where sensors, microprocessors, actuators, and networks work together to collect data, make decisions, and control devices **without constant human input.**
- **Types of automated systems:**
  - **Sensors:** detect and collect data from the environment like temperature, motion, light, and proximity (e.g. security alarms, automatic lights, parking assist).
  - **Controllers/microprocessors:** process input from sensors and run programs/algorithms to send commands to actuators.
  - **Actuators:** carry out physical actions based on commands (e.g. moving robot arms, heating boilers, speakers, and alarms).
  - **Communication networks:** allow different components to exchange information, either through wired connection (e.g. Ethernet, USB) or wireless connection (e.g. Wi-Fi, Bluetooth). This may include internet access for remote monitoring.
  - **Human–machine interface (HMI):** the way users interact with the system (e.g. touchscreens, buttons, mobile apps, and dashboards).

Embedded systems

Inputs
E.g. keyboard, mouse, microphone

Processing:
- Central processing unit (CPU)
- Graphics processing unit (GPU)

Outputs
E.g. monitor/screen, printer, speakers

Primary storage:
- RAM
- ROM

Secondary storage:
- Hard disk drive (HDD)
- Solid state drive (SSD)
- Optical (CD, DVD)
- Flash memory (USB stick, SD card)

Functions of automated systems
- **Data acquisition:** sensors collect real-world data (e.g. temperature, motion) and convert it into digital signals for processing.
- **Processing and decision-making:** a controller analyses data using programmed logic to make decisions (e.g. 'If temp. < 18°C, turn on heater').
- **Control:** sends signals to actuators to perform actions (e.g. a greenhouse system waters plants when soil is dry).
- **Communication:** transfers data and commands between components or to/from users (e.g. smart thermostat sends temperature data to a mobile app).
- **Feedback and adaptation:** the system monitors the effects of its actions using sensors. It may adjust behaviour based on feedback as **closed-loop control** (e.g. cruise control in a car adjusts speed based on terrain/incline).

Smart heating system	
Component	Role
Temperature sensor	Measures room temperature
Microprocessor	Decides if heating is needed
Actuator (heater)	Turns on/off heating
Network connection	Allows user to control via an app
HMI	Mobile interface for the user
Feedback loop	Monitors if the room reaches desired temperature

Memory and storage

Types of storage

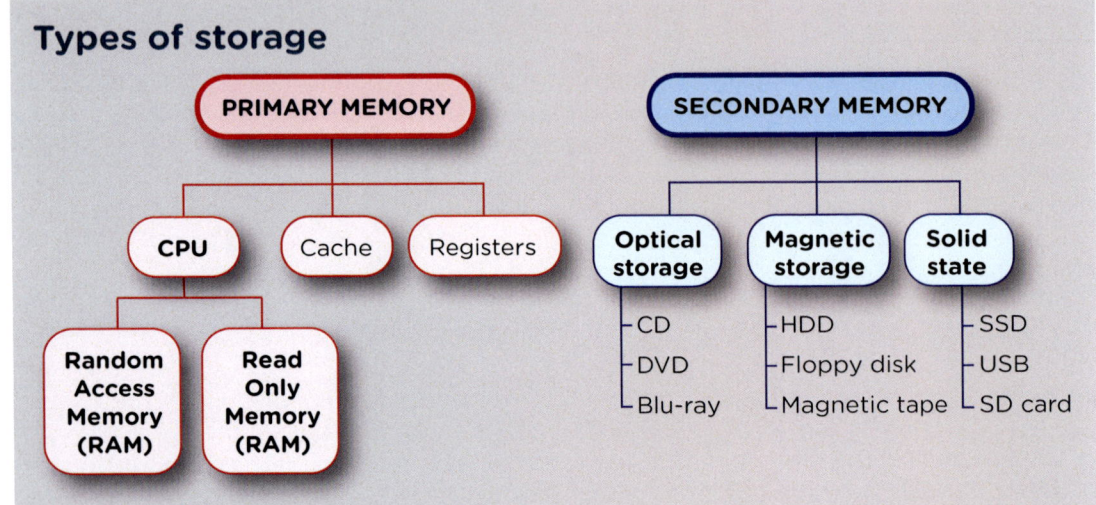

Units of data storage

- All data in a computer (text, images, sound, etc.) must be stored in binary (0s and 1s). Computers only understand on (1) and off (0) signals using electronic circuits.
- Increments of storage space go up in a geometric sequence (same multiplier), in this case ×2 (i.e. 1, 2, 4, 8, 16, 32...).
- **File size calculations:** to determine how much storage a file will need:
  - **Text file size** = bits per character × number of characters. There are usually **8 bits (1 byte)** per character (ASCII).
  - **Image file size** = colour depth × image width × image height. This is measured in bits. Colour depth = bits per pixel.
  - **Sound file size** = sample rate × bit depth × duration (seconds), often multiplied by the number of channels (e.g. 2 for stereo).

Unit	Size	
	Decimal	Binary
Bit	Smallest unit (0 or 1)	
Nibble	4 bits	
Byte	8 bits	
Kilobyte	1,000 bytes	1,024 bytes
Megabyte	1,000 KB	1,024 KB
Gigabyte	1,000 MB	1,024 MB
Terabyte	1,000 GB	1,024 GB
Petabyte	1,000	1,024 TB

Primary storage

- **Primary storage** is a computer's main memory, used by CPU to store program instructions and data while they are being processed. The two main types of primary storage are RAM and ROM.
- **RAM and ROM** both have direct access to the CPU, unlike secondary storage devices.

	RAM (Random Access Memory)	ROM (Read Only Memory)
Purpose	• Used for **temporary** storage of program instructions and data while being processed by the CPU.	• Used for **permanent** storage of program instructions and data, cannot have new data written to it. • Typically used to store the BIOS (Basic Input Output System) which is the boot-up sequence that loads the operating system from secondary storage into RAM as soon as the computer turns on.
Type of storage	• **Volatile:** data stored is lost when the computer is turned off or loses power.	• **Non-volatile:** data stored is not lost when the computer is turned off or loses power.
Notes	• Faster than secondary storage devices but more expensive per GB.	• Often made from flash memory which cannot be rewritten or added to without being reflashed.

Functions	ROM	RAM
Boots the system	Yes	No
Loads and runs programs	No	Yes
Permanent storage	Yes	No
Fast, temporary data access	No	Yes

Memory and storage

Secondary storage

- **Long-term storage:** stores program instructions and data until needed by CPU. This is provided by HDD, SSD, and optical media (CD, DVD). Common types of secondary storage include optical, magnetic, and solid state drives.

	Optical	Magnetic	Solid state
Examples	CD, DVD, Blu-ray	Hard Disk Drive (HDD)	SSD, USB stick, SD card
Capacity	Low (up to 50 GB)	Very high (TBs)	Medium to high (GBs–TBs)
Speed	Slow	Moderate	Very fast
Portability	High (small, light)	Moderate (portable HDDs)	Very high
Durability	Low (easily scratched)	Low (moving parts)	High (no moving parts)
Reliability	Moderate	Moderate	High
Cost	Very low	Low (cheap per GB)	High (expensive per GB)

	Advantages	Disadvantages
Optical	Cheap, portable, good for sharing or backups	Low capacity, slow, easily damaged
Magnetic	Large storage, affordable	Slower than SSDs, vulnerable to physical damage
Solid state	Fast access, durable, silent, energy efficient	Higher cost, limited write cycles (especially USBs)

- **Virtual memory** is a technique used by operating systems to extend primary/RAM storage when it is full by temporarily storing data from RAM sections (pages) in a file (pagefile) on secondary storage. This frees up RAM for other processes, enabling more programs to run simultaneously. However, since secondary storage is much slower than RAM, this can lead to reduced system performance.

Optical storage

- Optical storage (like CDs, DVDs, and Blu-ray discs) uses a laser to read data stored as tiny pits and lands on a disc's surface.
- Laser light reflects off lands (read as 1) and scatters off pits (read as 0). These patterns represent binary data.
- Blu-ray uses a blue laser to read smaller pits, allowing more data to be stored.
- This method allows data to be read quickly, but discs are easily scratched and have lower capacity compared to modern storage types.

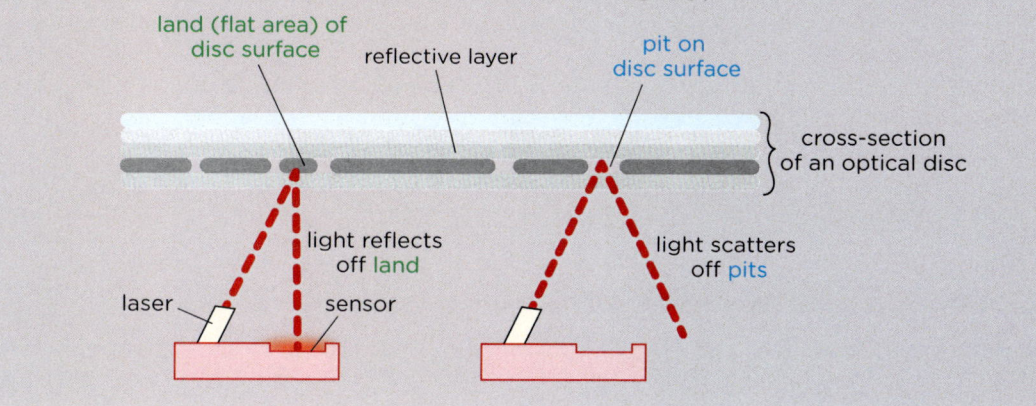

Magnetic storage

- Magnetic storage (like HDDs and magnetic tape) stores data as positive or negative magnetic charges, representing binary 1s and 0s.
- HDDs use spinning magnetic discs (platters) and a read/write head to access data quickly.
- Magnetic tape stores data on a long strip and reads it sequentially, making it much slower but ideal for large, long-term backups.
- Both are reliable and cost-effective, but HDDs are faster, while tape offers much higher capacity and durability for archival storage.

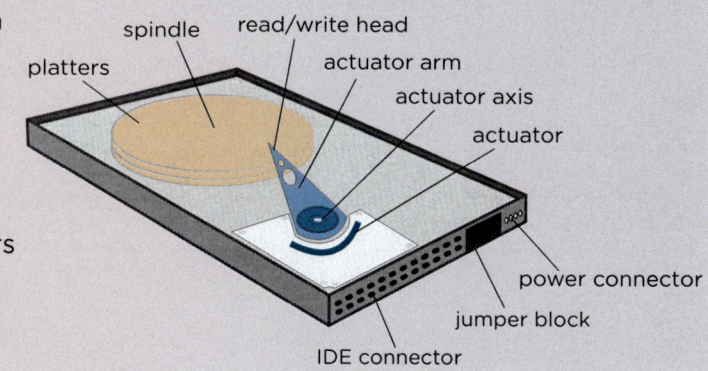

Number systems

Overview of number systems
- There are three number systems you need to know:
  - **Denary (decimal)** is the standard base-10 system used by humans, consisting of digits 0-9.
  - **Binary** is the base-2 system used by computers, consisting only of 0s and 1s; each binary digit (bit) represents an on/off or true/false state in hardware.
  - **Hexadecimal** is the base-16 system, using digits 0-9 and letters A-F to represent values 10-15; it provides a more compact and human-readable form of binary.
- Binary is used directly by computers, while hexadecimal simplifies the representation of binary values for programmers (e.g. colour codes, memory addresses).
- Conversions between denary, binary, and hexadecimal are common in programming, networking, and low-level computing tasks.

Converting between denary and binary (0-255)
- Binary is base-2 (0s and 1s). 8-bit binary is 8 digits (e.g. 13 = **00001101**). We convert by finding powers of 2 that add up to the number.
- For example, to convert the denary number **88** to binary:
  1. Start with the largest number that can be subtracted from 88 and give a positive integer (i.e. **88 - 64 = 24**) and put a **1** in that column.
  2. Take the remainder (**24**) and see if the next column can be subtracted from it (i.e. **24 - 32**). This would be a negative number, so put a **0** in that column and move to the next one.
  3. Repeat for the next column (**24 - 16 = 8**). This is positive, so put a **1**.
  4. Continue until there is no remainder (**8 - 8 = 0**) and put **0**s for any remaining columns.
  5. You can check your result by adding the place values for all columns with a **1** (i.e. **64 + 16 + 8 = 88** ✓).

Place values	128	64	32	16	8	4	2	1
Binary	0	1	0	1	1	0	0	0

- To convert a binary number to denary, add up all place values with a 1:
  - E.g. **10010111** = 128   0   0 + 16   0 + 4 + 2 + 1   = **151**
  - E.g. **00111100** = 0   0   32 + 16 + 8 + 4   0   0   = **60**
  - E.g. **11111111** = 128 + 64 + 32 + 16 + 8 + 4 + 2 + 1   = **255**

Converting between denary and hexadecimal (00-FF)
- Hexadecimal is base-16, using digits 0-9 and letters A-F.
- 1 hex digit = 4 binary bits.
- For example: **255** in denary = **FF** in hex.

Denary	0	1	2	3	4	5	6	7	8	9	10	11	12	13	14	15
Hex	0	1	2	3	4	5	6	7	8	9	A	B	C	D	E	F

- To convert hexadecimal to binary: multiply the value of the first digit by 16, then add the second digit (e.g. **D4** → D = 13 → 13 × 16 = 208 208 + 4 = **212**).
- To convert denary into hexadecimal: divide the number by 16 and use the integer as the first digit and the remainder as the second (e.g. **179** → 176/16 = 11.3 → 11 = B → first digit B, second digit 3 → **B3**).

Converting between binary and hexadecimal
- Split binary into groups of 4 bits:
- E.g. **11111111** = **FF** → **1111** = 15 (8+4+2+1), repeated → 15, 15 = **FF**.
- E.g. **10100011** = **A3** → **1010** = 10 (8+0+2+0), **0011** = 3 (0+0+2+1) → 10,3 = **A3**.

Binary addition
- Rules:
  - **0 + 0 = 0**
  - **0 + 1 = 1**
  - **1 + 1 = 1,0** (carry the **0**)
  - **1 + 1 + 1 = 1,1** (carry the **1**)
- 8 bit + 8 bit: e.g. **1000 1101 + 0100 1000**

```
    1 0 0 0 1 1 0 1
  + 0 1 0 0 1 0 0 0
  = 1 1 0 1 0 1 0 1
```
(1 carried over)

- **Overflow error:** happens when the result of a binary addition is too large to fit in the number of bits available (e.g. more than **255** in an 8-bit system). For example: **11111111** (**255**) + **00000001** (**1**)' = **100000000** needs 9 bits → overflow! This can cause incorrect results or crashes. To handle it:
  - Store extra bits (overflow) elsewhere in memory.
  - Set a flag bit to signal that an overflow occurred.
  - Software or CPU can detect the flag and break the sum into smaller, manageable parts.
  - Avoid continuing with faulty results.
- **Binary shifts**
  - Left shift: multiply by 2 each time (e.g. **00001010** → **00010100**)
  - Right shift: divide by 2 each time (e.g. **00010100** → **00001010**)

Encoding and compression

Characters
- A character set is a table that gives each symbol or letter a binary code.
- **ASCII:** 7 or 8-bit codes for basic English letters/symbols (e.g. A = 01000001, B = 01000010). This allows for 128 possible characters – mainly English letters, digits, and basic punctuation).
- **Unicode:** is much bigger than ASCII and supports many languages and symbols (e.g. Chinese characters, Arabic script, emojis) using more bits, typically 16, 32, or variable-length encoding like UTF-8.
  - UTF-8 is a popular Unicode encoding that remains compatible with ASCII for standard English text while allowing extra bytes for more complex characters.
  - Using Unicode enables global text processing, ensuring consistency and compatibility across platforms and languages.

Images
- Bitmap images are made of pixels, and each pixel has a binary colour code or colour value.
- Important terms:
  - Colour depth: bits used per pixel (more bits = more colours)
  - Resolution: number of pixels (width × height)
  - Metadata: info stored with image (e.g. dimensions, colour depth, file format, author/creator, camera details)

A high resolution image

A lower resolution image

Sound
- Sound is sampled at regular time intervals and stored in binary. A higher sample rate/bit depth means better sound, but a bigger file.
- Important terms:
  - Sample rate: number of samples per second (measured in Hz).
  - Bit depth: bits used to store each sample (e.g. 8-bit, 16-bit).
  - Duration: length of the sound in seconds.

Compression
- File compression reduces file size for faster downloads, saving storage, or streaming.
- Smaller files can load faster and transmit more quickly over networks. However, the trade-offs are that compression can reduce quality.
- There are two types of compression: lossy and lossless.
  - **Lossy compression:** removes data that humans are unlikely to notice (i.e. not visible/audible to our ears/eyes). For example, it may reduce colour detail and simplify areas of similar colour, so is suitable for photographs where perfect accuracy is less important.
  - **Lossless compression:** no data is permanently removed and the original image can be perfectly restored. This occurs through:
    - **Run-Length Encoding (RLE):** replaces repeated pixel values with a count (e.g. 10 red pixels)
    - **Dictionary-based compression** (e.g. LZW compression algorithm)

Type of compression	Lossy	Lossless
Quality	Some data is lost permanently	No data is lost
File size	Much smaller	Reduced, but not as much as lossy
Use	Images (JPEG), music (MP3), video	Text, software, images needing full quality
Advantage	Saves lots of space	Keeps original data exactly
Disadvantage	Can't get original back	Less space saved

Networks

Overview of networks

- A network is a collection of connected devices (computers, servers, printers, etc.) that can communicate and share resources.
- **Benefits:**
  - Enables easy file sharing (no USB sticks needed)
  - Facilitates shared resources: printers, scanners, internet
  - Allows for centralised management (e.g. to install updates or fix problems remotely)
  - Enables collaboration and communication across users
- **Risks:**
  - Security threats: hackers can access multiple machines
  - Malware spread: one infected device can spread viruses across the network
- **Factors affecting network performance:**
  - Number of connected devices/users (shared bandwidth)
  - Type of transmission media (wired is faster, more reliable, and less vulnerable to interference than wireless)
  - Physical obstacles blocking signals (walls, metal, etc.)

Client-server network model

- A network has servers and clients: the server provides services (e.g. files, websites, authentication), and the clients request and use these services. Examples of client-server networks include:
  - **File server:** stores and manages files
  - **Web server:** delivers websites
  - **Printer server:** manages print jobs
  - **Authentication server:** verifies usernames/passwords

Advantages of the client-server model	Disadvantages of the client-server model
• Central file storage accessible from any client • Central backups for all data • Central software/security updates • Team collaboration on shared documents • Central account management	• If the server fails, clients lose access • Costly server hardware • Single target for cyberattacks • Can be overloaded by too many requests (e.g. DoS attacks)

Peer-to-peer (P2P) networks

- Each device (peer) is equal with no central server. Peers connect directly to share files or stream content. Examples of P2P networks include:
  - AirDrop between iPhones
  - Streaming music to a Bluetooth speaker
  - Wireless printing
  - Sharing internet via personal hotspot

Advantages of P2P	Disadvantages of P2P
• Simple to set up • No costly hardware • No single point of failure	• No central management of updates • No central backup/security • Devices may be unavailable (switched off/disconnected)

Features	Client-server	P2P
Centralised server	Yes	No
Cost	More expensive	Cheaper
Setup complexity	More complex	Easier
Data backup	Centralised	Not centralised
File versions	Shared version	Multiple versions
Risk if 1 device fails	Server down = all fail	Still works

The cloud

- The cloud is a **remote service provision** meaning it delivers computing services over the internet instead of locally, hosted by worldwide data centres.
- Common services include data storage, software apps (SaaS), processing power, and hosting (e.g. Google Drive/Docs, Netflix, Dropbox, AWS).

Advantages	Disadvantages
• Access files and apps anywhere with internet • Scalable, secure back-ups/storage • Always updated software • No need for local IT maintenance	• Requires reliable internet • Less control over security • Potential for hacking • Unclear data ownership • Ongoing subscription costs

Networks

LAN and WAN
- **LAN (Local Area Network):**
  - Small geographic area (homes, schools, small businesses)
  - Owned and managed by the organisation
  - Can be wired, wireless, or both
- **WAN (Wide Area Network):**
  - Large geographic area (e.g. different cities or countries)
  - Used by multinational companies
  - The internet is the largest WAN
  - Telecom companies usually own the infrastructure

Network hardware (LANs)
- **Network Interface Controller (NIC):**
  - Provides the bridge between a device and a network.
  - Can be wired (RJ45 Ethernet port) or wireless (radio transmitter/receiver for WiFi).
  - Nowadays this is usually integrated into the motherboard.
- **Switch:**
  - Connects multiple devices to form a wired network.
  - Learns MAC addresses to forward data securely only to intended devices.
  - Supports star topology.
  - Can connect with other switches to increase devices on network.
- **Router:**
  - Connects different networks (e.g. home LAN to the Internet).
  - Uses IP addresses to determine where to send data packets.
  - Key for packet switching on the Internet.
  - Often combined with switch and wireless access point in home broadband routers.
- **Wireless Access Point (WAP):**
  - Connects wireless devices to a wired network via a switch.
  - Broadcasts the WiFi network's SSID (network name).
  - Uses encryption (WPA2-PSK) and authentication to prevent unauthorised access.

Transmission media

Type	Use	How data is transmitted	Bandwidth	Interference	Distance
Twisted-pair copper	Wired LAN connections	Electrical signals over copper wire	Up to 10 GB/s	Twisted pairs reduce interference	Up to 100 meters
Fibre-optic cable	Long-distance, high-speed WAN	Pulses of light through glass fiber	Up to 100 TB/s	No interference	Over 100 km
Radio waves	Wireless (WiFi, Bluetooth)	Electromagnetic radio signals	Up to ~300 MB/s (variable)	Prone to interference from other signals	Around 60 meters (affected by obstacles)

Components required for internet connection

Component	Purpose
Modem	• Modulates/demodulates signals between digital (your device) and analogue (telephone lines or fibre) • Connects local network to the internet service provider (ISP)
Router	• Directs data between your network and the wider internet • Assigns local IP addresses
Switch	• Connects multiple devices in a local area network (LAN) • Uses MAC addresses to forward data only to the intended device, reducing unnecessary traffic and managing data flow
WAP (Wireless Access Point)	• Provides Wi-Fi access to wireless devices • Connects to a wired network

- These devices work together: modem connects to ISP → router handles traffic → switch shares connection locally → WAP enables wireless access.

The internet

The internet and the world wide web

- **Internet:** a global **network of networks,** connecting millions of devices using standard communication protocols (TCP/IP).
  - It uses Internet Protocol (IP) addressing to send data, and routers move packets across interconnected networks.
  - You can think of it as a road network where the internet is the physical infrastructure (i.e. cables, routers, wireless connections) that carry many types of traffic (i.e. web pages, emails, file transfers, streaming). Without the internet's roads, no digital data could move between devices.
  - Uses of the internet include:
    - Hosting websites
    - Email and secure file transfers
    - Voice and video calls (Skype, Facetime)
    - Streaming services (video/music)
    - Cloud computing and storage
- **World wide web:** a collection of websites and web pages hosted on servers and accessed via the internet using web browsers.
  - It uses HTTP/HTTPS to communicate.
  - You can think of this as the vehicles that use the highways (cars, trucks, and buses) each carrying content (text, images, videos) to and from destinations. The Internet provides the **pathways** for information to move, and the world wide web provides the **content** that travels along those pathways.
  - **Web hosting:** websites are stored on web servers, and hosting companies charge fees based on bandwidth usage. They provide security, backups, and uptime guarantees.
- **Functions of a web browser:**
  - Bookmarks/favourites: save and access sites quickly.
  - User history: record of visited sites.
  - Multiple tabs: open multiple sites in one window.
  - Cookies: store data like login info or preferences.
  - Navigation tools: back, forward, refresh buttons.
  - Address bar: enter and display URLs.

Accessing the internet

- **Uniform Resource Locator (URL):** the address of a resource (e.g. page, image, video) on the web (e.g. https://www.example.com:443/path/page.html?user=123#section2).

Component	Example	Purpose
Protocol	https://	Defines how to connect data between your browser and the server
Domain name	www.example.com	Identifies the website/server
Port [optional]	:443	Specifies communication channel used by the protocol (usually hidden as browsers use default ports: 80 = HTTP, 443 = HTTPS, 21 = FTP)
Path	/path/page.html	A directory that locates resources on the server
Query string [optional]	?user=123	Sends additional parameters or data, often used in searches or form submissions
Fragment [optional]	#section2	Jumps to a section within the page

- **HTTP and HTTPS:**
  - HTTP (Hypertext Transfer Protocol): is used to transfer webpages and resources (HTML, images, etc.) over the web.
  - HTTPS (HTTP Secure): is the same as HTTP but with encryption via SSL/TLS. Used for secure transactions (e.g. shopping, banking). Always use HTTPS when sensitive data (e.g. passwords, card info) is involved.
- **Domain Name System (DNS):**
  - Translates domain names (like www.google.com) into IP addresses.
  - DNS servers query other DNS servers if they don't have the requested address.
- **How web pages are located and displayed:**
  1. URL entered into browser.
  2. Browser contacts a DNS (Domain Name Server) to translate the domain name (e.g. www.bbc.co.uk) into an IP address.
  3. Browser sends an HTTP/HTTPS request to the web server hosting the site.
  4. Web server responds by sending back the HTML code.
  5. Browser renders the HTML and displays the web page to the user.
- **Cookies:** small text files stored by a web browser to remember user data and preferences; often subject to privacy regulations (e.g. the General Data Protection Regulation (GDPR) in the EU), so users may be asked to accept or reject cookies.
  - **Session cookies:** are temporary and are deleted when the browser is closed (e.g. tracking cart items while shopping).
  - **Persistent cookies:** are stored long-term (e.g. login details or user preferences).

Network topologies

Star topology

- Network topology refers to how devices are arranged and connected to each other in a network. Note that topology refers only to the physical layout, not the network type (i.e. any topology can be peer-to-peer or client-server).
- A star topology is where devices connect indirectly through a central switch or hub. The layout looks like a star with connections radiating from the center.

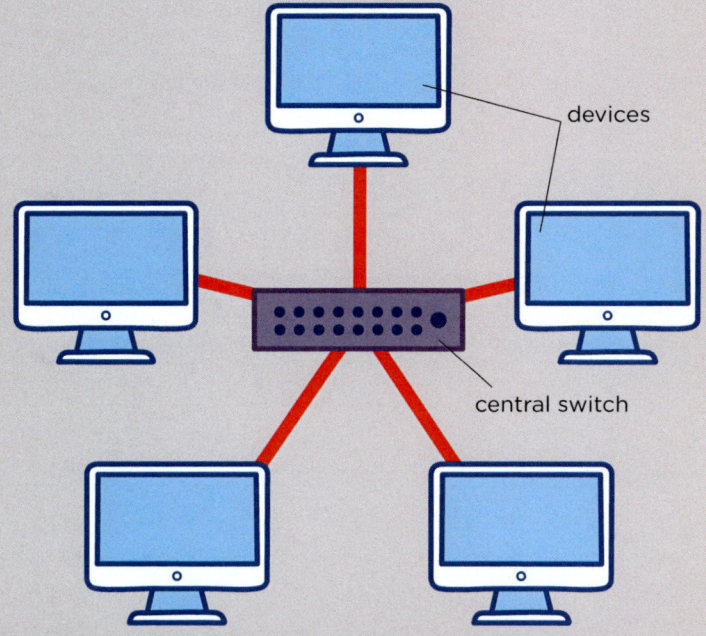

Advantages	Disadvantages
• Failure of one device doesn't affect the rest of the network. • The switch prevents packet collisions by managing data flow. • The switch can screen and discard corrupted packets, improving security. • Easy to add new devices.	• The entire network fails if the central switch fails (single point of failure). • Can be expensive to install because each device requires its own cable to the central switch.

Mesh topology

- A mesh topology is where devices connect to each other directly or indirectly without a central switch.
  - **Full mesh:** every device is connected to every other device directly.

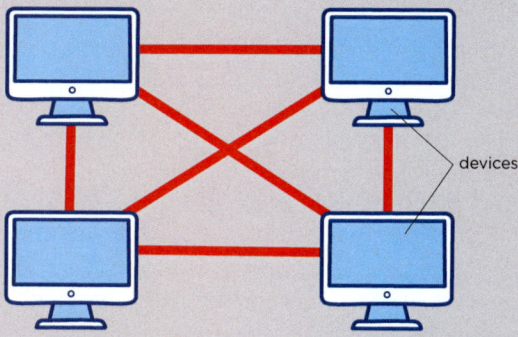

  - **Partial mesh:** some devices are connected directly, others communicate indirectly.

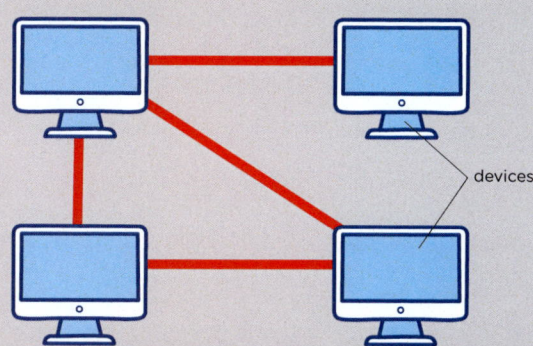

Advantages	Disadvantages
• No single point of failure, making it very robust; if one device fails, data routes via other devices. • Good for wireless networks where devices can relay data and extend network range.	• Wired mesh networks are expensive and complex, requiring many cables and interfaces. • Without a central control point, it's hard to monitor and secure all data traffic efficiently.

Wired and wireless networks, protocols, and layers

Modes of connection
- **Wired:**
  - Uses physical cables such as Ethernet (twisted-pair copper cables with RJ45 connectors).
  - Ethernet cables transmit data via electrical signals.
  - Typically faster and more secure due to direct physical connection.
- **Wireless:**
  - Uses **Wi-Fi** or **Bluetooth** radio waves to transmit data without cables.
  - Wi-Fi connects devices to wireless access points that broadcast an SSID, whereas Bluetooth is for short-range device communication.
- **WiFi frequency bands and channels:** WiFi uses radio waves to transmit data, primarily over two frequency bands: 2.4GHz and 5GHz.
  - The **2.4 GHz** band contains 13 channels, each spanning 22MHz, but most channels overlap, leading to signal interference. Only 3 channels (1, 6, and 11) are non-overlapping, limiting performance in crowded environments.
  - The **5 GHz** band contains 24 non-overlapping channels. This allows for more networks to operate simultaneously with minimal interference.
- **Encryption:**
  - Wireless networks use encryption to secure transmitted data. This prevents unauthorized users from reading wireless transmissions.
  - **WPA2-PSK** (Wi-Fi Protected Access 2 - Pre-shared Key) is the most secure means of authenticating devices on wireless networks.
- **Standards:** a set of agreed rules or specifications that ensure compatibility between hardware and software from different manufacturers. Without standards, devices wouldn't work together properly.

IP and MAC addressing
- **IP address:** a unique logical address identifying a device on a network used to route data to the correct device across different networks.
  - **IPv4 format:** 32 bits long, consisting of 4 numbers between 0–255 separated by dots (e.g. 192.168.1.1).
  - **IPv6 format:** 128 bits long, consisting of 8 groups of 4 hexadecimal digits separated by colons (e.g. 2001:0db8:85a3:0000:0000:8a2e:0370:7334).
- **MAC (Media Access Control) address:** a unique physical address assigned to a network interface card (NIC). It identifies a device within a local network and is used by switches to forward data to the correct device.
  - **Format:** six pairs of hexadecimal digits (e.g. 00:1A:2B:3C:4D:5E).

Protocols
- A protocol is a set of rules for sending and receiving data on a network.

Common protocols	Uses/description
TCP/IP (Transmission Control Protocol/Internet Protocol)	The fundamental protocols for sending data over the Internet; TCP ensures reliable transmission, and IP routes data packets
HTTP (Hyper Text Transfer Protocol)	Protocol used by web browsers to request and receive web pages
HTTPS (Hyper Text Transfer Protocol Secure)	Secure version of HTTP that uses encryption (SSL/TLS) to protect web data
FTP (File Transfer Protocol)	Protocol used to transfer files between computers on a network
POP (Post Office Protocol)	Protocol used by email clients to download emails from a mail server
IMAP (Internet Message Access Protocol)	Protocol that allows email clients to access and manage emails on a server without downloading them permanently
SMTP (Simple Mail Transfer Protocol)	Protocol used to send emails from a client to a server or between servers

Layers
- Network communication is structured into layers, each performing a specific functions and passes data to the next layer.
- Layering simplifies network design, helps isolate problems, and allows different technologies to work together. For example:
  - **Application layer** uses protocols like HTTP, FTP, SMTP.
  - **Transport layer** uses TCP to ensure reliable communication.
  - **Internet layer** uses IP to route data.
  - **Network access layer** handles physical transmission (Ethernet, Wi-Fi).

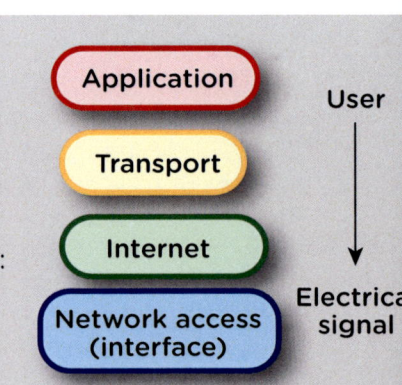

Threats to computer systems and networks

Forms of attack

- **Malware:** malicious software installed without user knowledge.
  - Purpose: disrupt, damage, steal data, demand money, or spy.
  - Types:
    - Viruses: infect host programs, damage files when run.
    - Worms: self-replicate without host, spread across networks
    - Trojans: disguised as useful software; trick users into installing.
    - Ransomware: encrypts files, demands payment to unlock.
    - Spyware: monitors user activity, e.g. keylogging.
    - Rootkits: modify OS to hide from antivirus.
    - Backdoors: open secret access for future attacks.

- **Social engineering:** tricking people (usually the weakest link) into giving access or data.
  - Purpose: gain sensitive information without technical hacking.
  - Types:
    - Phishing: fake emails/websites collect login info and passwords.
    - Cold-calling: impersonators ask users to 'confirm' credentials.

- **Brute-force attacks:** guessing passwords through automated tools. They will typically use 'dictionary attacks' first by going through common word and number combinations, then trying every possible combination, attempting millions of guesses per second.
  - Purpose: gain unauthorised access by cracking passwords.

- **Denial of service (DoS) attacks**: overwhelms a server with too many requests.
  - Purpose: disruption, blackmail, protest, or competitive sabotage.
  - **DDoS (Distributed DoS):** use multiple machines (botnet) to crash or slow down services, making them inaccessible.

- **Data interception and theft:** stealing data while it is in transit.
  - Purpose: identity theft, industrial espionage, or unauthorised access
  - Types:
    - Packet sniffing: reads data packets in transit.
    - MITM (Man-in-the-Middle): intercepts between user and server.
    - Insider attacks: trusted users steal data.

- **SQL injection:** a hacker inserts malicious SQL code into a form input, making the website unknowingly treat the input as a command. For example, a website may have an SQL query like 'check USERNAME matches PASSWORD.' If an attacker types 'OR 1=1,' then the query would be 'check USERNAME OR 1=1' and since 1=1 is always true, they can bypass login requirements.
  - Purpose: gain access to data without logging in properly.

- **Insider attacks:** a person within the organisation misuses access to sell, leak, or steal sensitive info for financial gain, espionage, or as a whistle-blower.
  - Purpose: data theft or sabotage from someone credible or trusted.

- **Passive attacks:** eavesdropping on network traffic without affecting it. This uses tools like packet sniffers which are hard to detect as they don't alter data flow.
  - Purpose: surveillance and gathering sensitive data quietly.

- **Active attacks:** direct interference with systems. Examples include malware installation, DoS attacks, brute-force, or MITM.
  - Purpose: disruption, control, or theft.

Threats to computer systems and networks

Identifying vulnerabilities

Prevention methods	What it prevents	How it works
Penetration testing	• Identifies security flaws, social engineering weaknesses, poor recovery planning.	• Simulates real attacks to test defences • May test users' susceptibility to scams and ability to recover after attack
Network policies	• Enforces good security practices across users and devices	• Sets rules for passwords, access, software, backups, testing, and firewall use to reduce vulnerabilities
Network forensics	• Helps trace and analyse past attacks to prevent repeats	• Monitors and stores traffic • Analyses unusual activity to find attack source and improve security strategy
Anti-malware software	• Blocks/detects/removes malware (e.g. viruses, backdoors, spyware)	• Uses signatures and behaviour-based detection • Scans files and running apps • Quarantines threats
Firewalls	• Blocks DoS attacks, spyware, external hacking attempts, and malware data leaks	• Inspects network traffic • Uses filtering rules (packet, IP, port-based) to block harmful packets or data leaks
User access levels	• Prevents unauthorised access, software installation, and insider misuse	• Assigns permissions to groups/users so they can only access necessary files/features, limiting accidental/malicious use
Passwords	• Protects against unauthorised access and brute-force attacks	• Should be strong, long, secret, and regularly changed • Weak on their own but useful with other methods
Encryption	• Protects data in transit and storage from being read if intercepted	• Scrambles data using large prime number based keys • Only decryptable with the correct key • Used in VPNs, WPA2, etc.

Preventing vulnerabilities

Threat	Prevention methods
Malware	• Anti-malware • User access levels • Firewalls • Network policy
Phishing / social engineering	• Penetration testing (tests staff) • Network policy (training, restrictions) • Passwords
Brute-force attacks	• Passwords (strong and regularly changed) • Firewalls (limit access attempts)
DoS attacks	• Firewalls (packet filtering, port blocking)
Data theft / interception	• Encryption (scrambles data) • User access levels • Firewalls
SQL injection	• Penetration testing (simulates injection attacks) • Network policy
Insider threats	• User access levels, firewalls (data leak blocking) • Network policy

Operating systems and utility software

System software
- **System software** controls the hardware in a computer and provides an environment (or platform) for application software to run.
- **Types of system software:**
  - **Operating systems (OS):** manage the computer's hardware and provide the interface and services for other software to run.
  - **Device drivers:** small programs that tell the OS how to use a piece of hardware (e.g. printer, mouse).
  - **Utility software:** programs designed for maintenance tasks like freeing up storage space or scanning for problems.

Functions of operating systems
- **Memory management and multitasking:**
  - Allocates RAM to different applications.
  - Ensures processes don't interfere with each other's memory.
  - Enables multitasking by allowing multiple programs to run at once.
  - Controls which process gets CPU time and how much.
- **User interface (UI):** allows the user to interact with the computer. There are two types of UI:
  - Command Line Interface (CLI): text-based (e.g. Command Prompt, Terminal)
  - Graphical User Interface (GUI): visual (e.g. WIMP – Windows, Icons, Menus, Pointer)
- **Peripheral management (device management):**
  - Manages external devices like printers, keyboards, and webcams.
  - Uses device drivers to communicate with hardware.
  - Keeps track of device connections and ensures correct data transfer.
- **User management:**
  - Controls which users can access the system and applies access rights (e.g. admin vs. standard user).
  - Each user has a username and password, and associated personal settings, files, and apps. User Access Control prevents unauthorised actions (like installing apps).
- **File management:**
  - Manages files on secondary storage (e.g. hard drive, SSD).
  - Handles actions like naming, saving, moving, and organising into folders, as well as tracking file locations, types, and permissions.
  - Ensures only authorised users can read (open), write (edit), and execute (run) files.

Utility system software
- **Encryption software:** prevents unauthorised access to files and protect sensitive files/drives from unauthorised users (e.g. in case of theft or hacking).
  - Uses an encryption algorithm to "scramble" data.
  - Only users with the correct key can decrypt and access the data.
  - Often works on-the-fly with the operating system (e.g. BitLocker, FileVault).
- **Defragmentation utilities:** improve hard disk performance by reorganising fragmented data.
  - Moves file fragments so each file's data is stored in adjacent blocks.
  - Groups free space together to reduce future fragmentation.
  - Makes file access faster and reduces wear-and-tear on the disk.
  - Not used with SSDs (Solid State Drives) as they have no moving parts and defragging can shorten their lifespan.
- **Backup utilities:** create copies of data that can be restored in case of data loss.
  - Can be either a full or incremental backup.
  - Full backup includes all data but takes longer and uses more space. This is typically scheduled (e.g. weekly or monthly).
  - Incremental backup includes only files that have changed (i.e. newly created or recently edited) since the last backup. This is quicker and uses less space.
- **Compression utilities:** reduce the size of files, saving storage space and making data transfer more efficient.
  - Uses lossless compression algorithms to shrink files without losing data.
  - Can compress many files/folders into one archive (e.g. .zip, .rar).
  - Often includes password protection for security.
  - Also allows decompression or extraction of files for access.

Impact of technology on society

Ethical, legal, cultural and environmental impact *(All specs except: CIE)*

- **Ethical issues:** concerned with what is considered right or wrong in the use and development of technology, even if it is legal.
  - Companies tracking online activity can improve services and personalisation but raise concerns about consent, transparency, and exploitation of user data.
  - AI replacing jobs may increase efficiency and reduce costs, but can lead to unemployment, de-skilling, and the need to rehire or retrain workers later.
  - Facial recognition technology in public spaces can improve security and crime prevention but risks loss of anonymity, bias in algorithms, and racial profiling.
  - Automation and decision-making by algorithms raise ethical questions about accountability when systems make mistakes.
- **Legal issues:** concerned with what is allowed or prohibited by law to protect individuals, organisations, and data.
  - Copying music, films, or games illegally (piracy) breaches copyright law and denies creators fair payment.
  - Hacking into systems is illegal under computer misuse laws and can result in data theft, fraud, or system damage.
  - Misusing personal data can breach data protection laws, such as collecting data without permission or sharing it unlawfully.
  - Laws also regulate acceptable online behaviour, including cybercrime, online harassment, and fraud.
- **Cultural issues:** concerned with how technology changes communication, work, lifestyles, and values across different societies.
  - Social media influences global culture by spreading trends, language, and ideas quickly across countries.
  - Technology can widen the digital divide, where people in poorer or rural areas have limited access to devices or the internet.
  - Increased screen time can change daily habits, reducing face-to-face interaction and affecting health and wellbeing.
  - Remote working and online learning can change traditional working and educational cultures.
- **Environmental issues:** concerned with technology's sustainability and impact on the natural environment.
  - E-waste from old computers, phones, and tablets can cause pollution if not recycled properly.
  - Data centres consume large amounts of electricity, contributing to carbon emissions if powered by non-renewable energy.
  - Mining rare metals for device components can damage ecosystems and use significant energy and water resources.

Legislation relevant to Computer Science *(Only: OCR)*

- **Data Protection Act 2018:** controls how organisations collect and use personal data. This Act states that people have rights to:
  - Know what data is held
  - Ask for their data to be changed or deleted
  - Have their data used fairly, lawfully, and securely
- **Computer Misuse Act 1990:** makes certain unauthorised activities illegal, such as:
  - Gaining access to computer systems without permission
  - Spreading malware
  - Carrying out denial of service (DoS) attacks
- **Copyright, Designs and Patents Act 1988:** protects creators (e.g. authors, musicians, developers) and prevents others from:
  - Copying or distributing work without permission
  - Claiming someone else's work as their own

Licenses and legal issues *(Only: OCR, Edexcel, Pearson IGCSE)*

- **Software licences:** control how software can be used and shared.
- **Open source software:** free to use, edit, and share, with its source code being visible and modifiable. Examples include Linux and GIMP. Open source licenses are popular for developers building custom tools as they can easily edit and adapt the code or crowdsource new features and solutions.
  - Benefits: encourages collaboration and allows for greater customisation.
  - Drawbacks: may lack official support or updates.
- **Proprietary software:** paid and legally owned by a company, so users cannot see or change the source code. Examples include Microsoft Office and Adobe Photoshop. Proprietary software is popular within institutions like government departments or schools that require reliable and secure services.
  - Benefits: generally reliable and well-supported (e.g. updated versions, customer support, consumer protection)
  - Drawbacks: costly, no ability to modify the software.

Computational thinking

Key terms for algorithms

- **Algorithm:** a clear, step-by-step set of instructions designed to solve a problem or complete a task. Algorithms must be precise, unambiguous, and finite. Generally, algorithms follow an **input-process-output** sequence:

Concept	Definition	Example
Input	Data received by the program	A user's age typed into a form
Process	Actions performed on the data	Calculate the user's birth year
Output	Result displayed or returned	Showing the user's birth year on screen

- This sequence can also be split into the following categories:
  - **Sequence:** instructions executed in a specific, fixed order. Every algorithm relies on sequence as a basic control structure.
  - **Iteration:** repeating a set of instructions until a condition is met. This includes count-controlled loops (e.g. FOR) and condition-controlled loops (e.g. WHILE).
  - **Selection:** making decisions within an algorithm based on conditions. This often involves using IF, ELSE, or CASE statements.
- **Decomposition:** breaking tasks down into smaller chunks, to make them easier to understand and solve.
- **Abstraction:** simplifying tasks by removing unwanted/unnecessary information and creating general solutions.
- **Pattern recognition:** the ability to recognise patterns in data and to build algorithms to make use of them, allowing solutions to be reused or applied more efficiently.
- **Logic:** using reasoning to determine the correct sequence of steps in an algorithm. This often involves true/false conditions and logical operators.
- **Flow diagrams:** a diagrammatic representation of an algorithm using standard symbols that help to visualise sequence, iteration, and selection.
- **Pseudocode:** a structured, English-like way of writing algorithms that is not tied to any specific programming language.
- **Validation:** checking that input data is reasonable and within expected limits. This prevents incorrect or harmful data from being processed.
- **Efficiency:** how well an algorithm uses time and memory. More efficient algorithms solve problems faster or with fewer resources.

Searching algorithms

	Method	Use case	Example
Linear search	Check each item in the list one by one until the target is found	Small or unsorted data sets	Searching for 7 in [4, 2, 7, 9]: → Check 4, 2, then 7
Binary search	Look at the middle item. If it's not the target: • Go left if the target is smaller • Go right if it's bigger • Repeat until found or list is empty	Large, sorted data sets	Searching for 6 in [1, 3, 5, 6, 8, 9]: → Middle is 5 → go right → 6

Sorting algorithms

	Method	Use case	Example
Bubble sort	Repeatedly compare and swap adjacent elements until the list is sorted	Small or nearly sorted lists	[4, 2, 3] → compare 4 & 2 → swap → [2, 4, 3] → swap 4 & 3 → [2, 3, 4]
Merge sort	Split the list in half until each part has one element, then merge pairs back together in order	Large lists needing efficient sorting	[6, 3, 9, 1] → split → merge sorted halves → [1, 3, 6, 9]
Insertion sort	Build the sorted list one element at a time by placing each element in the correct position	Small or nearly sorted lists	[4, 2, 5] → Insert 2 before 4 → [2, 4] → Insert 5 after 4 → [2, 4, 5]

Algorithm representation

Pseudocode
- This is a way to write algorithms in structured English.
- It is not actual code – instead it is designed to be easy to read while providing a basic understanding of an algorithm's function.
- Pseudocode is used to plan and design algorithms before writing actual code as it helps programmers focus on logic without worrying about syntax errors.
- Commonly used logical structures in pseudocode include: **IF, ELSE, WHILE, FOR, INPUT, OUTPUT**, etc.

```
INPUT number
IF number > 0 THEN
        OUTPUT "Positive"
ELSE
        OUTPUT "Not positive"
ENDIF
```

Structure diagrams
- A structure diagram shows how a larger problem is broken down into smaller subproblems or modules. It represents the hierarchy and flow of control in a program.
- Structure diagrams have a top-down design with each module performing a single, defined task.
- These diagrams are useful for debugging, reusing code, and understanding complex systems.
- For example, the structure diagram on the right shows a workflow for processing student data including inputs, processes, and outputs.

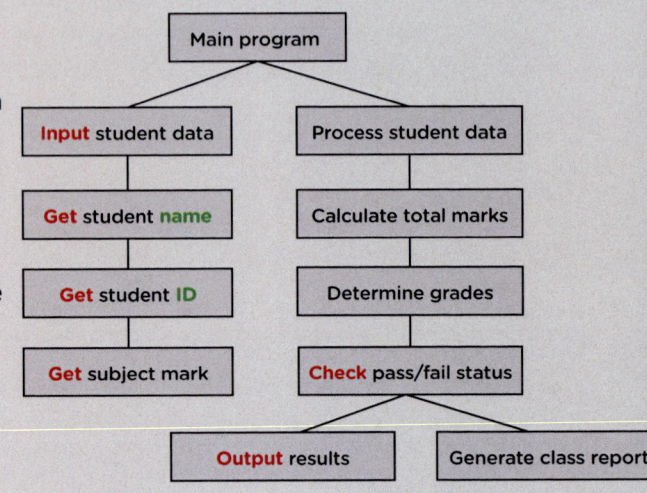

Flow diagrams
- Flow diagrams are used to visually explain a process (algorithm) and flow of information.

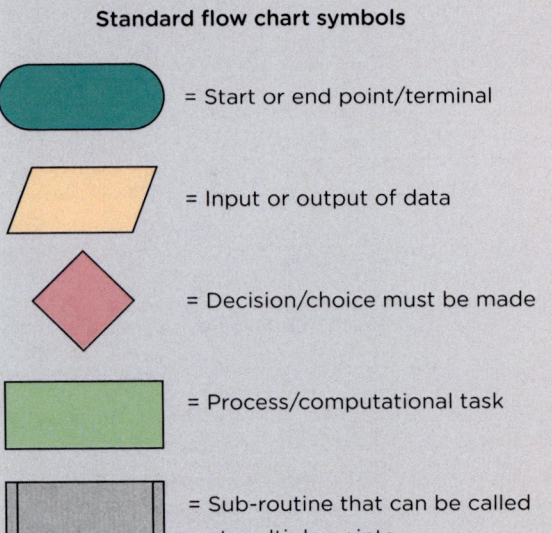

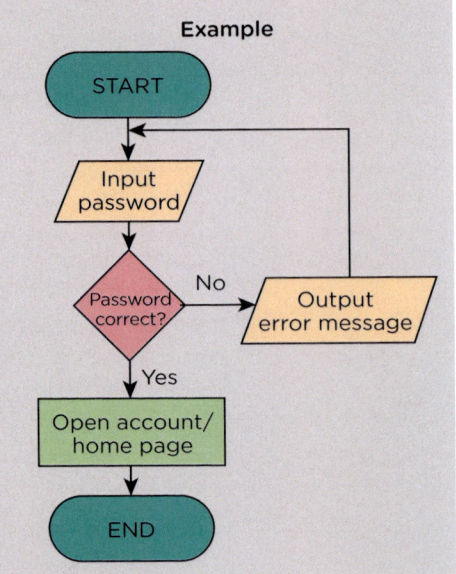

Nesting in algorithms
- Nesting refers to putting one control structure inside another for more complex algorithms with multiple layers of decision-making or repetition.

	Method	Use case	Example
Nested selection	One selection statement is placed inside another. The inner condition is only checked if the outer condition is met.	Tests multiple related conditions, checks input in steps (e.g. username correct, then password correct)	`IF x > 0 THEN IF x < 10 THEN ...`
Nested iteration	One loop runs inside another. The inner loop completes for each cycle of the outer loop.	Comparing arrays and performing large repetitions	`FOR i = 1 TO 5: WHILE condition ...`

Types of data

Standard data types

A data type defines the kind of data a variable can hold. Choosing the correct data type is essential for storing data efficiently, using appropriate operations, and avoiding errors.

- **Integer (int):** whole numbers (positive or negative), but cannot contain decimals. For example, 5, -100, 0. These are used when we need to count things or do mathematical calculations with whole numbers.

```
age = 16
```

- **Real (float/real):** numbers that can have decimals; sometimes called floating-point numbers (e.g. 3.14, -0.01, 100.0). These are used when dealing with things like prices, heights, or averages that require decimal precision.

```
price = 4.99
```

- **Boolean (bool):** only two values: True or False. This is useful when making decisions or checking conditions (e.g. if something is on/off).

```
logged_in = True
```

- **Character (char):** a single letter, digit, or symbol (e.g. 'A,' 'z,' '9,' '#'). These are used when we only need to store one character, such as a gender code ('M,' 'F').

```
last_name_initial = K
```

- **String (str):** a sequence of characters in the form of multiple letters, numbers, or symbols (e.g. 'Hello,' '123,' '@user!'). These are used when storing names, messages, passwords, etc.

```
username = "student_6685"
```

Casting (type conversion)

- Casting is the temporary conversion of one data type to another. It is required when a value's current type is not suitable for an operation.
- It allows for operations between different data types, and ensures we get user input in the correct type.
- User input is usually stored as text (string), even if it looks like a number, but mathematical operations cannot be performed on strings, so casting ensures data is in the correct format for processing.
- For example, in Python:

```
# Convert string input to integer
age = int(input("Enter your age:"))


# Convert integer to string
age_str = str(age)


# Convert string input to integer
price = 4.99
whole_price = int(price) # 4
```

- Explicit casting is when the programmer manually converts a data type using a function like int(), float(), str(), or bool().
- Implicit casting happens automatically without programmer instruction (e.g. combining an integer and a float results in a float).
- Numerical calculations require input to be cast to int or float. Failure to cast correctly can cause runtime errors.
- Numbers must be cast to strings when combining with text. This prevents type mismatch errors during output.
- Value errors occur when conversion is not possible (e.g. text to number).
- For Boolean values, non-zero numbers usually convert to True, and zero or empty strings convert to False.

Programming fundamentals

Key terms in programming

	Definition	Example
Variable	A named storage location that holds a value which can change during program execution	Value = 2 Value = 5
Constants	A value that does not change once set during the program (in Python, constants are written in uppercase)	PI = 3.14159
Input	Data entered by the user	name = input("Enter your name:")
Output	Information displayed to the user	print("Hello", name)
Assignments	Storing a value in a variable using the = symbol	x = 5
Syntax error	An error caused by breaking the rules of the programming language	Missing a colon at the end of an if statement in Python

Arithmetic operators

- These are used to perform mathematical calculations on numerical data and are essential for algorithms involving totals, averages, or counters.

Operator	Name	Example	Result
+	Addition	3 + 2	5
-	Subtraction	5 - 3	2
*	Multiplication	4 * 2	8
/	Division	10 / 2	5
MOD	Modulus (remainder)	10 MOD 3	1
DIV	Quotient (whole number division, no remainders returned)	10 DIV 3	3
^	Exponentiation	2 ^ 3	8

- In Python:
  - MOD is written as % (e.g. 10 % 3)
  - DIV is written as // (e.g. 10 // 3)
  - ^ is written as ** (e.g. 2 ** 3)

Comparison operators

- These are used in conditions (e.g. in if or while statements) and always produce a Boolean result (True or False).

Operator	Meaning	Example
==	Equal to	x == 10
≠	Not equal to	x ≠ 10
<	Less than	x < 10
≤	Less than or equal	x ≤ 10
>	Greater than	x > 10
≥	Greater than or equal	x ≥ 10

Boolean operators

- These are used to combine or modify multiple conditions.
- Boolean operators allow for more complex decision making:
  - AND: both conditions must be True
  - OR: at least one condition must be True
  - NOT: reverses the Boolean value; useful for checking the opposite of a condition
- Conditions are often grouped using brackets for clarity.

Operator	Meaning	Example
AND	True if both conditions are true	x > 5 AND x < 10
OR	True if at least one is true	x > 10 OR y == 3
NOT	Reverses the condition	NOT(x == 5) True if x is not 5

Programming techniques

String manipulation

- **String:** a sequence of characters (letters, numbers, symbols). Strings are written inside quotation marks. In Python, strings are immutable (meaning they cannot be changed directly).

```
name = "Ada"
message = "Hello"
```

- **Concatenation:** joining two or more strings together.

```
= "Ada"
"Lovelace"
first_name + " " + last_name  # "Ada Lovelace"
```

- **Indexing:** each character has an index number, starting from 0.
- **Slicing:** extracting parts of a string using indexes. This is used for extracting initials, substrings, etc.

```
word = "computer"

print(word[0])   # C
print(word[3])   # p
print(word[-1])  # r

print(word[0:4]) # Comp
print(word[3:])  # puter
print(word[:8])  # Compute

print(len(text))    # 8
```

Other common methods of string manipulation are:
- `upper()` and `lower()` to change to uppercase/lowercase.
- `strip()` to remove spaces
- `find()` to locate a character or substring. This returns the index of the first match, or returns -1 if not found.

File handling

Operation	Description	Python example
Open	Open a file (in `r` = read mode, `w` = write mode, or `a` = append mode)	`file = open("data.txt", "r")`
Read	Read content from a file	`data = file.read()` or `file.readline()`
Write	Write to a file (overwrites)	`file = open("data.txt", "w")` `file.write("Hello")`
Close	Closes the file	`file.close()`

Records

- A record is a collection of related fields (like a row in a table).
- Each field can be a different data type.
- Records group related data under a single structure. This is useful for storing information about people, books, products, etc.

```
student = {
    "name": "Alex"
    "age": 16
    "grade": "B"
}
```

Structured Query Language (SQL)

- SQL is used to access and manipulate data in a relational database (i.e. tables) made up of rows (records) and columns (fields).

SQL keyword	Description	Python example

SELECT	Choose which fields (columns) to display	`SELECT name, age`
		 `FROM students`
		 `WHERE age >= 16`

FROM	Choose the table to search	
WHERE	Set conditions to filter results	

- For example, if we wanted to: "Select all names from the 'books' table where genre is 'Sci-Fi' in alphabetical order," then our SQL entry would be as shown on the right.

```
SELECT name
FROM books
WHERE genre = "Sci-Fi"
ORDER BY name DESC
```

Programming techniques

Arrays (lists)
- **1D arrays:** store one list of items (e.g. names, scores)
- **2D arrays:** are arrays within arrays – like a table (rows and columns). 2D arrays are useful for emulating database tables (rows = records, columns = fields). Remember that the first row and column will be indexed as 0.

```
# 1D array
names = ["Kai", "Toby", "Adika"]
print (names[1]) # Kai
```

```
# 2D array
students = [
    ["Kai", 16, "A"],
    ["Toby", 17, "C"],
    ["Adika", 16, "B"]
]
print (students[0][2]) # A
```

Random number generation (RNG)
- RNG can be used to add unpredictability in programs which is useful for things like games and simulations.
- You must import the **random** module to use this.

```
import random
number = random.randint(1, 100)
        # Random no. between 1 and 100

dice = random.randint(1, 6)
print(dice)    # Random no. between 1 and 6
```

Subprograms
- Subprograms are blocks of code that can be called and reused. They make code more structured and readable.
- A subprogram is called by its name and passing required arguments. You can call a subprogram multiple times to avoid repeating code.
- There are two types of subprograms:
  - **Functions:** return a value.

```
# Function example
def add_numbers(a, b):
    total = a + b
    return total
```

  - **Procedures:** perform an action but do not return a value.

```
# Procedure example
def def print_grade_report(name, marks):
    # Calculate average
    total = sum(marks)
    average = total / len(marks)

    # Determine grade
    if average >= 80:    grade = "A"
    elif average >= 70:  grade = "B"
    elif average >= 60:  grade = "C"
    elif average >= 50:  grade = "D"
    else:                grade = "F"

    # Print the report (no value returned)
    print("Student Name:", name)
    print("Marks:", marks)
    print("Average:", average)
    print("Grade:", grade)

# Calling the procedure for multiple students
print_grade_report("Kai", [85, 90, 88])
print_grade_report("Toby", [32, 40, 29])
print_grade_report("Atika", [67, 81, 73])
```

- **Local variables:** are declared inside the subprogram and only used there.
- **Global variables:** are declared outside the subprogram and are accessible anywhere.

```
x = 10           # Global variable

def change_local():
    x = 5        # Local variable
    print(x)

change_local()   # 5
print(x)         # 10 (global x unchanged)
```

- Arrays (lists in Python) can be passed to subprograms as parameters. The subprogram can process all elements of the array (e.g. finding totals/averages, or searching for values),

```
def print_average(marks):
    average = sum(marks) / len(marks)
    print("Average:", average)

student_marks = [70, 85, 90, 60]   # Array

# Calling the procedure
print_average(student_marks)       # Average: 76.25
```

Producing robust programs

Defensive design
- Defensive design is about writing programs that can anticipate problems before they happen – especially incorrect inputs or misuse.
- **Anticipating misuse:** users might enter invalid, unexpected, or malicious input. The program should handle this without crashing.
  - Examples of misuse include typing letters into a number input, leaving fields blank, and entering a script or code (e.g. for hacking)
  - This can be addressed by using input validation, using authentication (to check who the user is), or displaying error messages and ask for correct input
- **Authentication:** is used to verify a user's identity, typically using:
  - Username + Password
  - Sometimes 2FA (two-factor authentication)
- **Input validation:** checks that the user's input is acceptable before using it in the program. Validation prevents bugs and improves security.

Common types of checks	What it does	Example
Length	Checks input is not too short or long	Password length >= 8
Range	Ensures number is within limits	Age between 0 and 120
Type	Checks if input is the right type	Number not string
Format	Pattern is correct	Email contains @
Presence	Ensures input is not empty	Name is not blank

```
# Authentication example
username = input("Enter username:")
password = input("Enter password:")

if username == "admin"
and password == "1234"
    print("Access granted")
else:
    print("Access denied")
```

```
# Age validation example
age = input("Enter your age:")

if age.isdigit():
    age = int(age)
    if age >= 0 and age <= 120:
        print("Valid age")
    else:
        print("Age out of range")
else:
    print("Please enter a number")
```

Maintainability
- Maintainable code is easy to read, update, and debug – even by someone else.
- **Use of subprograms:**
  - Break code into functions or procedures.
  - Each does one clear task.
  - Makes the code reusable and easier to test.

```
def get_user_input():
    name = input("Enter your name:")
    return name
```

- **Naming conventions:**
  - Use meaningful names for:
    - Variables (user_name, total_score)
    - Subprograms (calculate_tax, check_password)
  - Avoid: x, abc, thing1 (unless used temporarily or in loops).
- **Indentation:**
  - Shows which code belongs inside loops, conditions, or subprograms.
  - Python requires indentation (usually 4 spaces).
  - Helps with logic clarity and avoiding syntax errors.

```
if score > 10:
    print("High score")
```

- **Commenting:**
  - Comments explain the code, especially what it does and why something was done a certain way.
  - Good comments help other programmers (and your future self).

```
# To calculate total price with tax
def calculate_total(price):
    return price * 1.2
```

Testing programs

Purpose of testing
- To ensure a program works as intended and meets its design requirements
- To identify errors early, reducing time and cost of fixing them later
- To check that a program produces correct and expected outputs
- To improve the reliability and robustness of a program
- To support the refinement of algorithms by revealing weaknesses or inefficiencies
- To improve accuracy and user experience

Types of test data
- You must understand and be able to distinguish between four main types of test data to make sure your validation checks work properly.

Type	Description	Example
Normal	Data that is expected and valid	Age: 25 (if range is 0–120)
Boundary	Data at the edge of valid input	Age: 0, 120
Invalid	Correct type, but outside valid range	Age: -1, 130
Erroneous	Wrong type of data	Age: "twenty" (string instead of integer)

- **Selecting suitable test data:**
  - Must include normal, boundary, invalid, and erroneous values
  - Chosen based on the rules and constraints of the problem
- **Test plans:** are tables showing: test data, the expected result, the actual result, and a Pass/Fail outcome. These are mainly used in final testing to provide evidence the program works correctly.

Types of testing and test plans
- **Iterative testing:**
  - Carried out throughout development.
  - Each module or section is tested as it's written.
  - Helps identify and fix errors early.
  - Useful for things like testing a login function before integrating it into the whole system.

```
# Iterative test example
def square(n):
    return n * n

print(square(4))
```

- **Final/terminal testing:**
  - This happens at the end of development and tests the entire system to make sure everything works.
  - Final testing simulates real-world use and is an essential last stage of development.
  - For example, on the right and below is a final test and a test plan for age validating access to a children's activity centre for 5–12 year olds:

```
# Final test example
def check_age(age):
    if age < 5 or age > 12:
        return "Rejected"
    else:
        return "Accepted"
```

Test data	Type of test data	Expected result	Actual result	Pass/Fail
7	Normal	Accepted	Accepted	Pass
5	Boundary	Accepted	Rejected	Pass
12	Boundary	Accepted	Accepted	Fail
4	Invalid	Rejected	Rejected	Pass
18	Invalid	Rejected	Rejected	Pass
"ten"	Erroneous	Rejected	Program error	Fail

This tells us we have made a logic error with the upper bound

This tells us we have made a syntax error with handling erroneous data

Types of errors
- **Syntax errors:**
  - Break the rules of the language, meaning the program won't run (e.g. misspelled keywords ('pritn' instead of 'print'), missing punctuation, or incorrect indentation).

```
pritn("Hello")    # Syntax error
```

- **Logic errors:**
  - Occur when the program runs but gives wrong results, caused by incorrect algorithm structure or flawed reasoning in the code (e.g. using >= instead of >, or an incorrect loop range).
  - These can be harder to find because there are no error messages.

```
age = 10
if age > 18:
    print("Child")    # Logic error
```

Designing, creating, and refining algorithms

Trace tables

- Trace tables are tools used to manually follow the steps of an algorithm and track the value of variables at each stage.
- They are useful in spotting logical errors and understanding how an algorithm works.

```
x = 0
FOR i = 1 TO 3
    x = x + i
NEXT i
OUTPUT x
```

i	x
1	1
2	3
3	6

Final output: 6

Amending algorithms

- On the right is an example of a program to identify whether a user's test score is above a threshold of 50%.
- If we needed to amend this algorithm to account for a new requirement, such as checking for scores above 90 to be awarded a distinction, then we could add the following:

```
# Original algorithm
score = int(input("Enter score:"))

if score < 0 or score > 100:
    print("Invalid score")
elif score >= 50:
    print("Pass")
else:
    print("Fail")
```

```
# Amended algorithm
score = int(input("Enter score:"))

if score < 0 or score > 100:
    print("Invalid score")
elif score >= 70:
    print("Distinction")
elif score >= 50:
    print("Pass")
else:
    print("Fail")
```

Refining algorithms

- Turning a designed algorithm into executable code requires the correct syntax and an accurate translation of logic.
- Refining an algorithm can involve:
  - Improving an algorithm after testing it
  - Fixing logic or adding validation
  - Optimising performance or clarity
- For example:
  - Original code doesn't check for empty input → add a condition to handle it.
  - Original algorithm uses multiple nested ifs → simplify with elif.
- Refinement is often based on test results. More refined algorithms be easier to read and maintain but may have more or fewer steps depending on whether more specificity or efficiency is needed.

```
# Original algorithm
age = int(input("Enter age:"))
print("Age recorded")

# Refined algorithm
age = int(input("Enter age:"))

if age < 0 or age > 120:
    print("Invalid age")
else:
    print("Age recorded")
```

```
# Original algorithm
numbers = [2, 4, 6, 8]
total = 0

for i in range(0, len(numbers)):
    total = total + numbers[i]

print(total)

# Refined algorithm
numbers = [2, 4, 6, 8]
total = sum(numbers)

print(total)
```

Boolean logic

Logic gates and symbols

- Boolean logic is used in computer systems to make decisions using only two states: **1 = True**, and **0 = False**.
- It is based on logic gates and Boolean operators: AND, OR, and NOT. These are used in logic diagrams, truth tables, and real-world decision-making in code and digital circuits.

Operator	Description	Symbol (logic gate)
AND	True only if both inputs are true	(AND gate symbol)
OR	True if at least one input is true	(OR gate symbol)
NOT	Reverses the input (True becomes False, and vice versa)	(NOT gate symbol)

- Logic diagrams show how logic gates are connected. You need to be able to:
  - Recognise AND, OR, and NOT symbols.
  - Draw diagrams from expressions.
  - Trace how inputs flow through each gate.
- Tip: work from left to right and evaluate gate-by-gate when solving a diagram.
- Alternative notations you may see:

Symbol	Meaning
∧	AND
∨	OR
¬	NOT
T	True (1)
F	False (0)

Truth tables

- Truth tables show all possible input combinations and their result when a logic operator is applied.
  - **AND (A ∧ B):**

A	B	A ∧ B
0	0	0
0	1	0
1	0	0
1	1	1

  - **OR (A ∨ B):**

A	B	A ∨ B
0	0	0
0	1	1
1	0	1
1	1	1

  - **NOT (¬A):**

A	¬ A
0	1
1	0

Combining operators

- You may be asked to evaluate or draw logic diagrams with multiple gates, such as **(A AND B) OR (NOT C)**.
- For example:

A	B	C	A ∧ B	¬ C	Final output
0	0	0	0	1	1
0	0	1	0	0	0
0	1	0	0	1	1
0	1	1	0	0	0
1	0	0	0	1	1
1	0	1	0	0	0
1	1	0	1	1	1
1	1	1	1	0	1

Programming languages

High-level vs low-level programming languages
- High-level languages are easier for **humans**.
- Low-level languages are closer to **machine instructions**.

Feature	High-level language	Low-level language
Closer to	Human language	Machine (CPU) language
Example languages	Python, Java, C#, JavaScript	Machine code, assembly
Ease of use	Easier to read and write	Harder to read and write
Portability	Portable across systems	Not portable (CPU-specific)
Control over hardware	Less control	Direct hardware control
Used for	Software development	Embedded systems, device drivers
Needs translation?	Yes (via compiler/interpreter)	Yes (machine code may not)

Translators
- Computers can only understand machine code (binary), so programs written in high-level or assembly languages must be translated into machine code.
- The two main types of translators are compilers and interpreters. For example, Python uses an interpreter which is good for rapid development, whereas C# uses a compiler which is good for performance and deployment.

Feature	Compiler	Interpreter
Translation style	Translates entire program before running	Translates and runs line-by-line
Speed	Faster after compilation	Slower overall
Error detection	Shows all errors at once	Stops at the first error
File type produced	Creates a separate executable file (.exe)	Does not produce an executable
Examples	C, C++ (compiled)	Python, JavaScript (interpreted)
Memory usage	Uses more memory initially	Lower initial memory usage
When to use	Good for large, finished programs	Good for testing, debugging, development

The Integrated Development Environment (IDE)

Only: OCR, Edexcel, Pearson IGCSE

- An IDE is a software application that provides a range of tools to help programmers write, test, and debug programs more efficiently, all in one place.
- **Editor:** a code-writing window where you type and edit your program.
  - Helps by making code easier to read, write, and understand.
  - Often includes features like syntax highlighting (e.g. keywords in colour), line numbers, auto-indentation, and code suggestions/autocomplete
- **Error diagnostics (debugger):** helps you find and fix bugs in your code.
  - Identifies syntax errors (e.g. missing brackets) and logic errors (e.g. incorrect conditions).
  - Can show error messages, line numbers where errors occur, and/or suggestions for corrections.
- **Run-time environment:** allows you to run your program inside the IDE without needing a separate compiler.
  - Helps by letting you test your program as you develop it, and observe how it behaves with real inputs.
  - May support step-through execution, where you run code line-by-line to see how it behaves.
- **Translators:** built-in tools that convert your code into machine code.
  - Helps by making your program executable by the computer.
  - May include a compiler (translates the whole program) and/or an interpreter (runs the program line by line).

Python

Key features of Python

- Python is a high-level programming language that is widely used for:
    - Software development
    - Web applications
    - Data analysis
    - Machine learning
    - Automation

Feature	Explanation
Easy to read	Python uses simple English-like syntax making it more beginner-friendly.
High-level	No need to worry about low-level details like memory management.
Interpreted	Python code runs line by line, making it easier to test and debug.
Versatile	Can be used for web development, game creation, data science, AI, etc.
Large community	Lots of tutorials, libraries, and support available online.

- Python uses indentation to define blocks of code (e.g. loops and selection).
- Incorrect indentation causes syntax errors.
- Statements are usually written one per line. Semicolons are not needed.
- **Variables and data types:**
    - A variable stores data and is created using the assignment operator =.
    - Common data types:
        - **int** – whole numbers
        - **float** – decimal numbers
        - **str** – text (strings)
        - **bool** – Boolean values (True or False)
- **Iteration (loops):**
    - **for** loops are used when the number of repetitions is known.
    - **while** loops repeat while a condition is true.
    - **break** can stop a loop early; **continue** skips to the next iteration.

Basic structure of Python

- **Variables and data types:**

```
name = "Kai"          # String
age = 16              # Integer
height = 1.68         # Float
is_student = True     # Boolean
```

- **Input and output:**

```
name = input("Enter name:")
print("Hello", name)
```

- **Control flow:**

```
# If statements
if age >= 18:
    print("Adult")
else:
    print("Child")

# For loops
for i in range(5):
    print(i)

# While loops
count = 0
while count < 5:
    print(count)
    count += 1
```

- **Lists (arrays):**

```
fruits = ["apple", "banana", "cherry"]
print(fruits[1]) # Output: banana
```

- **Functions:**

```
def greet(name):
    print("Hello" name)
greet("Kai")
```

- **Operators:**

```
# Arithmetic
+    # Addition
-    # Subtraction
*    # Multiplication
/    # Division
//   # Integer division
%    # Modulus
**   # Exponentiation

# Comparison
==   # Equal to
!=   # Not equal to
>    # Greater than
<    # Less than
>=   # Greater than or equal to
<=   # Less than or equal to

# Boolean
and    # both True
or     # at least one True
not    # reverses value
```